T0365802

WE ARE NOT ALONE

AuthorHouse™
1663 Liberty Drive
Bloomington, IN 47403
www.authorhouse.com
Phone: 1-800-839-8640

Published by AuthorHouse 10/30/2014

ISBN: 978-1-4969-5013-0 (sc)
ISBN: 978-1-4969-5016-1 (e)

Library of Congress Control Number: 2014919376

Any people depicted in stock imagery provided by Thinkstock are models, and such images are being used for illustrative purposes only. Certain stock imagery © Thinkstock.

This book is printed on acid-free paper.

Because of the dynamic nature of the Internet, any web addresses or links contained in this book may have changed since publication and may no longer be valid. The views expressed in this work are solely those of the author and do not necessarily reflect the views of the publisher, and the publisher hereby disclaims any responsibility for them.

authorHOUSE®

We Are Not Alone

VOLUME 1

Pamela Ortega

PREFACE

I was born and raised in California. I have Native American ancestry. I live in a paranormal world every day. In this world, there are dragons, fairies, angels, unicorns, spirits, little people, wolves, vampires, witches, and UFOs, which I believe are biblical aliens. They are shape-shifters -they shape into any object. The different races of aliens are the Kemens, the Yemens, the Grays, and another -I couldn't make out the name.

There is a war going on right now over there, and some volcanoes are about to erupt. There are a lot of holes in our sky, and we are parallel to the aliens. They are like us. They understand English and speak it, and I'm sure they understand every language. They use their language as the old Roman language.

Treaties are made there -the aliens showed me, and they are real. Their planet has a shape of a man working with a hammer on it. It reminds me of our moon, how we have a shape of a man in the moon. They are into saving our lives and being reborn. They have something to do with the Anunnaki. They still use flying carriages; they use horses and wagons still. They showed me this with the photos and some goddesses, which I think are half gods. I believe they helped make the pyramids, from what they showed me.

Our astronauts said they were escorted to the moon by a UFO with domes on it. The ones with which I interacted look the same way. It's very interesting, the way they eat and the way they use their mathematical system.

The "Men in Black," I was told, are friendly, and they have been friendly with me. An important person -one of the Men in Black in their world -or a very well-liked one was killed; they showed me that. I have seen the Men in Black; they have long black trench coats. They are huge guys with bald heads. Three of them came walking toward me, and I do admit I got nervous, but they have been nice to me. They reassured me that they are friendly. So there are two kinds -some are bald, and some have hair and wear hats. I think they are from different races, because when they talk about the photos of the trees, which are like mazes, they usually put the letter *V* in every scene. They use numbers with letters. They write on my shirts, pants, carpet, and walls, in constant communication with spirits and my guardian, V, UFO, the paranormal.

ACKNOWLEDGMENTS

I'd like to thank my son for helping me at my worst (rest in peace), as well as a few acquaintances who helped me. Thank you so much, AuthorHouse, for the patience and understanding and for being considerate as I continue my journey.

INTRODUCTION

I was born with a gift, and now it is time for me to say what I see. I still am trying to understand what comes my way. I am the youngest of four children. One sister and one brother passed away at a young age. I was born and raised in Orange County, California, in a little city called Santa Ana, where everyone is somehow connected to everyone else -at least that's what I've noticed when I've checked out my family history. I am a Native American and have always been very intrigued with other worlds. I have always heard stories from my family about UFOs but never really read much about them. It just seems exciting to hear of them. At family weddings, we ask our uncles to tell us stories.

I've always believed in angels and saw them when I was seven. They were very huge, on the side of my house, as though they were praying for my family. I've seen some orbs and a few spirits. My mother always told me to be straight with the Lord, and that's what kind of pulled me from my journey. I was in my rebellion days -I got in some troubled and paid my price to society. I spent my twenties in California prisons but made it out for my twenty-fifth birthday.

So I'm here to say that people can change their own lives, if they put their minds to it. I believe this is a short life and that we are here for a reason. We each have a gift that God gave us. We just have to learn how to use it. If you are in prison or you're not doing too well, I'm here to tell you that you can still find your gift and use it, just as well as the other person. I don't believe in judging a book by its cover.

My father was a contractor, and my mother was a housewife. My father wanted to be a brain surgeon, but we needed food on the table, so like every middle-class family, Dad did what paid the bills -he went to construction and then became his own contractor. At one time, my mother and father saw a UFO on Chapman Street in Orange, California. My father said he would never forget it. It was two telephone poles high. My mother said it had red, blue, and green lights on it and around the flying object. There were about six people at the gas station at the time. They all looked at each other, all baffled. My mother later ran to the backyard, praying to the Lord for the world not to end so she could have her baby -she was pregnant at the time with me. They tease me, calling me VN1, the Seaweed Queen, because I can see them straight ahead of me. Their name is V-Aliens, the oldest aliens around and biblical.

CHAPTER 1

Back in 1986 or '87, my grandmother gave me her ticket to a retreat up in Riverside, somewhere in the San Bernardino Mountains. It was a weekend Christian retreat, where there would be prophets and Catholics. They had two huge pools, luncheons, and prayer for the day; it was really beautiful up there. I was very lucky that she gave me her ticket; she must have felt I needed it. I slept in a room with four other girls. Everyone was there for a wonderful weekend with the Lord, and boy, was I excited to hear them speaking in tongues. We ate on dining room tables covered with beautiful white cloth and shining silverware. They really went all out for that weekend; it was nice. I went swimming that afternoon and then joined the other girls for lunch. After that, everyone went to the prayer meeting.

Shortly after that, I went for a walk by myself in the mountains, and I prayed. I found an area with another pool, but the pool was dirty. I climbed up the mountain. I was always told the best place to get close to God was the mountains, and I was going to pray. It kind of reminded me of Fallbrook, where we use to live in San Diego on a farm. So there I was, praying, and after a minute or two, the dirty pool turned sparkling clean and clear. Fire came up the side of the pool, and it looked like there was grass in the middle of the pool and sparkling water on the sides, and with fire running on the side of that too. As I was looking at that sparkling pool and the burning fire, I suddenly saw a UFO, shaped like a sideways teardrop, going from tree to tree among the palm trees around the pool.

I could see the reflection of them when they shaped the trees. I saw that the UFO straight ahead through the first palm tree was a man on a horse. The other palm tree was an angel, with just a head and wings sticking out on the side, with a human face. The next palm tree was a cross that told me about soldiers for Christ. I could not believe what I was seeing; the water had gone from mud and mold to sparkling clean. And the fire -it was so beautiful. I just couldn't believe it. I knew that had to be from God or some kind of being, because of the UFO. I knew there was some kind of connection.

Later that day, after I ate, I was walking upstairs. There was a mirror on the wall, and I looked at myself. I noticed a yellowish color around my eyes, so I went to a lady and prayed with her. I'll never forget it; we prayed, and then she told me to walk back to my room without turning around. That night, I was very surprised at what I saw from my balcony: a blue UFO and a red UFO going up and down. There was a full moon that night, and I saw another palm tree right next to me at the balcony, flowing in front of the shining moon at the same time the UFO was flying up and down.

I was very excited. I couldn't wait to tell my father and mother what I had seen. Then I walked into the room from the balcony and saw the Bible. I opened it up and looked down. The first thing I read was, "You have seen what most prophets would have loved to have seen in a lifetime." I never wrote down the chapter, but yes, I did read that from the Bible.

The next morning, I went with a few relatives to luncheon and prayer. At the prayer, I broke down crying. A lady walked up to me and held me; she called another lady to come to her. I couldn't believe my eyes -it was the human face on that angel that I'd seen when I was praying up in the mountains. The lady holding me said, "Soldiers for Christ," just like the UFO. It was very interesting hearing about UFOs, but this was shaped like a sideways teardrop. Later, they sent me to a home, and they wanted to change the name of the home. It had vineyards in the backyard. I would walk up and down them and pray; a cloud would be forty or fifty feet above me, following me.

Everything was very nice, but I had to go to court, so I had to come back to Santa Ana.

Big mistake. I never returned to the home, but I started to go to Jewish temples. They were beautiful, and I started to see all kinds of things in the sky. I would ask people, "Do you see that? A lamb and people on horses." They would look at me like I was crazy. I went to a home and got a beautiful dress from the East that had Eastern writing on it. As I would yell to everyone to look at the sky, they must have thought I was going crazy. I did not think of getting a camera.

Maybe it was just not the right time to show people what I was seeing. This was in 1986 and 1987. I started seeing faces in plants -like another world -but no one else could see them or believe me. Again, I didn't think of a camera. I was still attending the Jewish temple. I would get the little hats and give them to my Gamma. My mother would get mad, because I didn't give any to her.

I continued to see things in the sky. Later, I went upstate, and maybe it was because I was close to a lot of reservations and my heritage is American Native, but they showed themselves to me. I was in Avenal, California, and I actually saw some Indians looking at me through the windows. I was lying down one afternoon on my bunk, and from my feet up, they started to float up in the air. I got up right away and looked around to see if anyone had actually seen. I did not want anyone to see me. Later, I was transferred to Stockton and locked down.

As I was in Stockton, a being came in my cell; it was very unusual. All the girls said I was hallucinating. Maybe so, maybe not, but as we go along my journey, it's coming together as I take one day at a time. It's kind of hard living in these parallel worlds. Then, when I was back at the California Institution for Women (CIW), I attended a Native American church. I wished I could have gotten into one of those sweat lodges, but I did not

CHAPTER 2

I saw an Indian in his regalia when I worked in the kitchen at Avenal State Prison. He was smiling at me, and my son was next to him with his arm out. He caught an eagle on his arm. They were both very happy, and so was I. I remember the stories my father always told me about his mother and him, and it would make my day. I was very happy to have visions like that.

Another time, we were walking through CIW after time in the yard, ready to be locked in. A beautiful white owl flew right over me. I took it as a good sign. When I saw something like that, it always reminded me of home and my father and mother and of the stories they told me. I've always kept them close to my heart, so it made me feel close to home.

I still saw faces everywhere -in the plants, the sky -but I stopped telling people to look. They would think I was crazy, but I know deep inside that it was real. These weren't just spirits; these were real.

The being in my cell looked like it was manifesting, like it was coming out of the wall. I'll never forget that, or the time my feet started to float up. I was placed in a lot of lifer cells and thought maybe I was seeing the spirits of the people they had killed who were still hanging around. If I had that kind of cell, I always said a prayer for the deceased. That was my own little ritual; I always made sure to do it, as that would always make me feel good before I continued talking to them or living with them.

Finally, when I got out, I stayed at my mother's. I was still seeing things but not really paying attention to them. But one night, I saw little men in my mom's backyard, and she saw them too. We were scared and called the police. My mother told me about orbs and auras and showed me how to clean my aura. One day I was cleaning my aura, and I showed my son how to clean his aura in the same way. He was my only son, may he rest in peace. My boy -I miss him so much.

My father would tell me stories of when he was nine or ten years old. He said he would help his mother and his aunts to levitate a table, He said, "Boy, oh boy, were they excited" -it worked much better when he helped them, and so they would oil him up. I think that was normal to them because my dad and mom were born on an Apache reservation, and their bloodline was Apache and Cahuilla. As a matter of fact, I'm working on determining their heritage. I took my paperwork to the Bureau of Indian Affairs (BIA). They asked for more paperwork, so I collected a lot of paperwork. My mother's grandmas and grandpas were all up and down the coast. My advice to anyone is to always look up your heritage. We would not be here if it weren't for our ancestors.

My father had a birthmark behind his shoulder; it's the same one I have on my leg. I always thought it looked like an airplane, because it looks like it has wings, so I've always been scared to go on planes.

CHAPTER 3

When I was ten years old. I had a dream of a plane crashing and a girl looking at me through fire. I had that dream for weeks at a time, and I would wake up screaming.

I remember a time when my mom was at church, but I was at home, sick, and my father was taking care of me. He opened up the baby aspirin, but the sound of turning the cap on the bottle scared me. I thought it sounded like fire when fire clicks. I haven't had that dream for a while now.

My father told me his mother once took him to a witch doctor. Two girl cousins and his aunts and mom went with him to Los Angeles to see this witch doctor. The witch doctor said that no witch could touch him because he was very powerful. On the way home, they crossed some railroad tracks, and a crow flew in front of their car. He told his mother to stop. He was so excited to get the crow and take it home, but when they got home, his father would not let him keep it. So he took it to his cousins' house and put it in a cage. He said he wrapped a chain around it, and he was just so excited. He could not wait for the next morning to go to the crow. When morning came, he was so shocked to see the crow was missing, yet the lock and chain were still wrapped around the cage.

He went inside to ask his aunts about the crow, and they said that the night had been so frightening for the girls. A man had flown into their room -the same witch doctor they had seen -and he was hovering over the girls' bed. He was wearing a black cloak and flying over them, so they said the crow was the witch doctor.

My father always told me to try to levitate, but I never have tried it. I always thought he was playing under the table, making it rise, but he actually was meditating with his mother. His aunts liked that it worked so well with him. but his mother stopped it, so there's always been a little mystery in the family -some people are not open-minded. They must think it's really bad and mysterious, but for someone who was born and raised on reservations, it's just a normal thing for them; it's everyday living with the Creator, which would be with the Lord to closed-minded people. He always told me we were here for a while, and we come back to reach our peak, to finish in life what we had not finished when we were here on earth. My mother also told me that we were just passing through, that this is not home.

Throughout my life, I have felt fast movement, where I have to hold to the walls. I've felt that maybe four or five times, it feels like everything is moving fast. One night I was walking in the kitchen, and the door flew off the wall. It flew right by me, and I ran back in the room. That wasn't as strange as the way I've been sleeping for the past four years -with my legs floating in the air. The knock on the door is a little song, a Mexican tune that my sister says is from the 1930s. A knock has other meanings, but I thought at the time it meant that a friend had passed away.

Later, I was arguing with someone, and everything went flying off the bathroom shelf. And then I got mad, and the bed shook. I talked to my sister, and she told me some incidents, and it confirm to me that it could be telekinesis. My father was moving things very heavy, like a car, when he was sick with colon cancer. He said he'd been doing it since he was a kid.

He also slept just like me (or I slept like him), with legs in the air. I guess some things run in the family. When I would tell him what I saw in the sky, he would tell me, "I believe we are not alone in this world." Space is too huge for just us.

He told me that his cousins wanted to get hypnotized, because they were abducted, and they couldn't stand the light. One had the most luck all the time, and the other ones were sick. The doctors could not diagnose them; they didn't know what they had. One day, the three of them were at the yard where they'd meet before going to work a construction site. One stayed by the truck, the other sat on a wooden fence, and one had to use the restroom, so he went to the side of the yard. When he came back, he wasn't walking. Some man was holding him. He said that he looked like a flat piece of wood. While the man was holding him, his feet weren't hanging down as they do when someone holds you, and the man was sliding.

The cousin that was using the bathroom came out through the side of the bushes, and a man was holding him. And the other cousin fixated on his feet, because the man was sliding like he was on an escalator. He said he was not walking; he just staring at his feet. He had a robe on. The man carrying him was sliding toward a pile of wood on the side, and he laid him down. He thinks they lost some time there, and until this day, they still talk about it. So there have been UFOs seen in our family for a while now.

My father went to the hospital for his equilibrium. I was at the hospital for my hospital insurance. I had no idea that my dad was in the hospital, but a friend and I were walking up to the car, and I started walking sideways. Could it be because we were so close, and I was feeling him that day? I don't know. I thought it was kind of strange.

CHAPTER 4

I lay down on the ground outside, looked up, and saw a whole different world. One day I started seeing flying saucers again, flying all over. No one would see them. Signs change. Everything is just so different. All my life, I've seen a white light wrapped around trees, and I never could make out what it was, but when the saucers came back, I stayed quite a long time. I didn't want to say anything to anyone. My mother always told me to ask them questions, to see what they wanted, but I would say, "Mom, they're flying around. It's not like I can just say, 'Hey, stop!'" She would just chuckle and say, "Okay, but they're here for something." I would tell her, "I know," but I still wouldn't push the issue,

I guess when I was ready to talk to them, I would. I asked everyone I was with if they could see them, but they couldn't see them. I wish sometimes that I could have gotten into the sweat lodges at CIW, but I didn't like to see the killers that got that beautiful actress. She controlled the other side of the church, and when I heard what she did to the actress and her baby, I did not like to listen to that. She was always there. Rest in peace to her and the others, but when I go through pictures, I see that they were always there with me, the whole time. They're so beautiful.

One morning, I told a friend that I'd had a lucid dream of an alien's baby. Aliens were playing in my room, driving little scooters in the air. They would fly their scooters above my bed. Playing, they would fly them down toward me, very close to my face, and then make quick U-turn. It was cute. I never felt threatened by them.

Another time when we redid our mobile home, we came back after being away, but the carpet wasn't in at the time, so the floor was a little cold. I felt someone tapping on my face, saying, "You're back; we missed you." I opened my eyes and at the window, I saw a light moving around, as if someone was out there, moving it -but no one was there. It was a good feeling. I just went back to bed. It reminded me of when my mother told me the there was a little girl spirit playing with the pots and pans in her kitchen, and it didn't bother her at all.

A few months later, I was watching TV. I heard a loud noise in the backyard, like a body or something was moving in the bushes. I got up to look, but nothing was there. I sat down to watch TV again, but there was the noise again. I ran to the door to catch whatever was there, but there was nothing. I told Danny, "I know I heard something out there, and there it goes again.

This time I ran to the door to catch what was making that noise, and I hid next to the door. There was a light moving around my front door in circles, like someone had a flashlight, moving it around. I stood sideways at the door, determined to catch whatever was there. When I stood sideways at the door to catch what was in the bushes, I looked through the window on the door -and I saw a whole family. I shook my head, and said, "No way; this can't be." I saw a family, like someone was rolling a film in front of me. It was like history playing in front of me. I called my mother and told her I saw people eating on a table, a man with a beard, and someone that even looked like my mother. That night, I woke up every hour on the hour, to see if this was real. Yes, it was real; it was still there. Orange groves were there. They showed me the pioneer days -it all flashed right in front of my eyes.

Danny's daughter came by, and she saw the same thing I did. She saw people going fishing, and people in striped clothes like they wore in the olden days when they put someone in jail. They were laying down a string down a hill and putting people down there. Then they were right from Ezekiel from the Bible. I'd been reading Ezekiel, and it kind of makes sense that they talked of certain objects in that chapter. They showed me different things. I went outside to look around one of my plants, and there was a perfectly round circle. A big round ball-shaped thing had landed in a bush. They pulled it out before I got a picture of it, but they also left "to AA" written on the front of my home.

I was bringing groceries in from the car, and as I walked by, I looked at the floor and said to myself, "Where have I seen those markings? Oh, on TV -that's a marking that some aliens leave when they land. I took a picture of it.

I still look at them every day. I don't say anything to them; I just stare at them.

CHAPTER 5

I called my mother, and she told me to talk to them.

I said, "No, though I think they understand me. It's like we are reading each other's minds." They would nod their heads and show me people picking trees in orange groves. And this place was full of orange groves before, so then I told myself that I would take photos of them. I started to take photos of them, and they were writing in their photos.

I met a man I call JC -he spelled his name like that, but I'm sure they called him Junior too. I decided that I would not take any more photos, but they started to put long fingers on the screens, and they were writing "VN1" to me. I looked it up; it means a "special person," all over the world. I tapped on the wall and said, "This is the last photo." I grabbed my camera, aimed to where the knocking came from, and there was a head, floating with high beams -like it would look through binoculars with lights. They printed on my shirt a photo of the print, as well as on my pants.

I started to follow up on what they were writing. It led me to a man in China. I still have to reach him. It's not so easy to just get a message. I was going through a lot. I didn't know who my friends were or who was following me. I called the news and wrote to the *Register* but got no answer. I'm still getting messages now, but when I received those messages at the time, it sent me to a Chinese man and our first astronaut, rest in peace, who landed on the moon. I think I was supposed to reach him, but I didn't, and I felt very bad that I didn't. But then I was so very happy that they showed me the ceremony held for him. What's strange is that the Chinese man is a professor who knows different languages. Everything was adding up.

Every day was so very exciting and still is. They showed me from the other side, and they told me I was queen. They started writing "sweet queen." They are so beautiful; they're like the movie *Close Encounters of the Third Kind*. They're like lights -they come out of these other saucers, and they all just fly around. They fly around the trees, and shape them, and write in the trees. They send messages and move the trees. I put a few on YouTube. If you look under "Pamela Ortega UFO Santa Ana, California," you will see them and the little people.

When I first saw them in the window, a light was in front of me in the window. It made faces. A little face came out and stuck out its tongue, and it smiled. After a while, though, I couldn't look into that light, or it would burn my eyes, That night, I got photos of all kinds of things -ghost flying in my living room, fairies, unicorns, and dragons. I could not believe what I was seeing. It was like history was passing right by me. Some of the time it showed things from the Holocaust, or it could it be from my past, or it was the other world.

I started taking more photos. And they would always shape the trees and write in them. It took me back to the retreat -the one for which my grandma gave me the ticket. That's when I first saw the UFO, flying; the one that was shaped sideways like a teardrop. When I think about it now, I remember that when I was a little girl, about seven years old, I would be on a swing and always saw a kangaroo in the riverbed. And I would always talk about a friend name Lena. Now, they are shape-shifters. Around the first week, I was seeing them. It reminded me of *Star Trek*, the TV series. A man came out of nowhere and appeared to me. He started talking to me by moving his mouth, like he wasn't sure how I spoke, so he moved his lips to the form of the word to see if I could hear him or understand him. He had a V carved on his forehead.

It was scary, because I didn't know if it was bad or good, but I had no bad feeling. Just imagine yourself looking in a window, and a man's head comes forward and starts talking to you. You wouldn't know what to imagine. So many things were going on. I felt later like I was paranoid, but I kept praying to our God, Lord Jesus Christ. I was raised that way, so I did, but I felt bad. And my mother taught me how to cleanse my aura, so that's exactly what I did.

CHAPTER 6

They showed me so many things. I saw meetings they had with certain presidents. I saw their cars or ships -their ships are shaped like a dinosaur. I would have dreams me, taking care of dinosaurs, And then, before my eyes, I saw people calling my name, holding banners, and saying, "We love you, Pam," and "She was a queen. They had a ceremony for her when she passed away." It was a whole world of its own, and I was their queen. They were so very sweet to me, except for my people. If people from our world talked, I didn't know if I could trust them.

At the same time, I was in the bathroom, and I saw people lined up -people that I knew. JC opened my ears and told me to be brave. I heard people talking. Someone said. "You mean Pam already knows?" So it must have been someone who had burned me. Now, they call me "VN1" -special person around the world -and their queen. I knew there would be a lot of groups attacking me. So no wonder JC told me to be brave.

Earlier that day, I saw the aliens. They were all lined up. They looked European. Some were young, and some were adults, and some were in their sixties. Suddenly, they changed into horses, and cows, and dogs, and a few dinosaurs and birds. And then, all of the sudden, their faces came back. I knew right away they were telling me that they were shape-shifters. They showed me a lot of meetings they had, and when they signed treaties, there was a few flags up -five on one side. On the other side, there were humans sitting in the auditorium, and a few security guards or spacemen in a uniform -red or white leather jumpsuits, with a V on the chest in the opposite color. Three men were dressed like that in the auditorium, and the others had glasses on. They were humans. There were three aisles going down the auditorium and nineteen rows of seats. All were full of kids, and there were families too. I saw two aliens -a young one and an older one. Their automobile was shaped like a dinosaur or a huge bird.

Someone was giving speeches all the time, one lady at a time. One had short hair, and they let me see her face. They had teaching classes with a lot of children. One little girl, I'll call her Pixie, had pigtails and always was making funny faces. She was so cute. She had freckles and red hair. She put her thumb in her mouth and blew her cheeks really big. She smiled and made cute faces -she was just too funny.

Now we were back in the spaceship, and there was a girl on the side, in a block of hay, writing on a chalkboard. She kept writing the same thing, over and over -and then there came the face again. Jeez, I was a little stunned, because I knew this was their boss. He had a V carved on his forehead. Then I was by a lake with three other people and a table, and a lot of people came out in a line. They were signing something, and I was directing. There was a lot of grass by the lake, like in a meadow. I wondered if it was their world or ours.

Then they showed four people walking, and then only one came at the end. I didn't know what that meant. Then they showed another meeting, and there was old man, showing me dolls. He moved them up and down, and I was trying to figure out what he was saying.

I figured he was trying to distract me. He didn't want me to look to the left. To my surprise, there was a meeting going on.

CHAPTER 7

I saw another race -a different nationality. When I was looking in I saw about seven of them, and three stepped up. Their faces were different, as if they had skin hanging from their faces. Then the next day, another group came in, as if they were making some kind of deal. These ones were a lot darker than the ones that had their skin falling off. It was like the Planet of the Apes. They were gorillas, talking. I could not believe my eyes. I figured their skin was different because of the environment of their planet. Their feelings are just like ours; they are just like us. Their world is like ours. As for the people's feelings and actions, there are bad people on earth and bad people on their planet. Not one is any different from us except their skin. They walk and talk like us -and they shape shift.

In one classroom, every time one of the gorillas would walk, two friends of mine -I call them my oracles -would roll their eyes at me, as if they were telling me, "Look who's here. Don't say anything." And the rest would put their heads down. I felt so sad for them. They protected me at one time, and I felt so helpless; I didn't know what to do.

I just had to stay quiet and wait until they left, but it happen like that sometimes. I wonder about the times that people see Bigfoot. It's just a spacecraft stopping in and the aliens walking around, because believe me, one came to my door, and it was kind of scary.

One day I was going to the store, and I saw a UFO. I said to myself, "I'm going to write about this." When I got home, a little face was looking in my window. He seemed to not know if there was an opening there. He had on a Roman war uniform and a sword. The uniform covered up his mouth. His face peeking in the window and he looked around, trying to see where I was. That was a sight to see. I hid right away. I got a feeling that I was at the wrong place at the wrong time. Then I saw this man was tied up. I thought it was my friend. What could I do? They had him tied up and pushed against the wall, with tape on his mouth. He was protecting me. I felt so bad that I wanted to cry. There I was again, not knowing what to do, feeling helpless again. That, to me, was telling me to not talk to him. I didn't see him for a while. They were gone for a minute, but they were always outside with me, to take their photos, and they always warned me of any harm coming my way.

I saw him in another section of the holes, and he had hay on him. I found out later that hay was good for them. Later, I saw the family that I first saw eating dinner -the same things I first saw when I started to see them. I don't know if it was a war going on over there, or if there was going to be a war down here. It was hard to understand, but it seemed like there was a war going on over there. By the first photos, there were two horses in the back of the gas station. One goddess was lying down on the horse with her legs hanging on each side of the horse. There was another horse and a goddess, and the goddesses were dressed in clothes from present time. She was hanging over the horse, and a huge man was hanging over her, with a spear through his back. Both goddesses were dressed in while Roman uniforms.

Later, at my home, I saw kids playing in my living room -a girl and boy, both about seven years old. There was a man who maybe was their father. They were playing with a dog. Also, a little girl was swinging on the front porch. JC told me there was a war going on over in their world -in V World -with three races. I'm not sure why they were fighting, but I saw how they would put down their heads when the gorillas walked in and had to bow to them until they left. They couldn't speak when they were there. They were sure looking at me when they walked in, so I wouldn't get their attention. They took very good care of me in that room for a while. It reminded me of a fantasy room. When they put up letters, sometimes they used birds. or when they sent Morse code, they used a little person to tap dance. One day when I was looking in the hole, I saw some kind of demon. I called a priest over to bless the house. What I noticed was that the gray aliens left, and a passive race stayed behind -the V biblical aliens.

I think that's why their orbs were blue, and when I first put it on YouTube, I didn't know what to do. At first, I figured, what if I get abducted or something else happens to me? So I talked to someone who convinced me to put them on YouTube to see how they took it, and their orbs turned red. They were a little disturbed by what I did, My lawyer also had a detective come over to take a photo of the hole. And they didn't want to show themselves, probably because of the way they would put on commercials -if you see an alien, shoot him. I think that is so wrong for our commercials to have that. They are just another race, like ours, but different because of the environment, By the look on their faces when the detective left, I felt like I betrayed them. They all gathered together and looked at each other.

CHAPTER 8

They had a look on their faces that seemed to ask what I was doing. I think that's why I got along with them for so long, because I didn't put them out there right away, and they knew they could ask me a question without having to run away. One day, I was praying, and they asked me why I prayed. I stopped and thought, *They're actually asking me.* Being comfortable, I told them I was raised to pray to our Lord Jesus Christ, God, and that most of our people prayed to our Lord.

They asked as if they were very curious and nodded their heads. Then I got a photo of their faces and of the passionate look they had. One looked like a possum and one had a face of a possum and a body of a turkey. Some look cute and friendly, and they cackled. I always saw them in the hole, but now I was on the porch. The cackle started, and then there was a serpent dragon. It quickly went up my legs, and its warmth healed a spider bite and a sore on my leg that night. It was kind of trippy, and looking at that demon, I called a priest to come over.

The demon had four horns, but his back was facing me on the rug in the living room. He was grabbing at some little people with his hands, so I said, "No way. You're not going to grab my little friends." That's when I called the priest, and when I looked in the hole, they had him cut up. His arms and legs were ripped apart, and they were tying him down. I was so excited to see that they got him. Then that night, the fairies came out. There were bar spirits that looked like sea creatures; they warn you of everything.

This paranormal man came over and mentioned them to me, and I said, "Yeah, they're always here." He said that people call them dumber spirits, that they look like sea creatures. One fairy was green -a little green man with wings on him. He just was so green. I was out taking photos, and when we had to go, I didn't turn my camera off. I thought I did, but it was meant to be. When I was getting in the car and moving my hand, I caught on tape a little pie-pan shaped saucer with a little man in it.

I was so surprise to get that photo by accident. Then, later that night, they showed a little city of people going to work, and they were moving fast on escalators. They were holding suitcases, and it looked like everybody was going to work -it was a sight to see. There was this other section where they slid down a section like a slide. A bunch of people were sliding down and up, like a roller coaster. Then, another day, I was coming home, and I said to myself, "I wonder how the spaceship looks." All of sudden, a portal came down, two houses down from me. A portal is a transfer port that spaceships use to transfer their bodies to and from. I never went to see because I was nervous. I never wanted to approach the portal because I thought I could be abducted. They've been okay with me so far, but one time I got nervous because I saw a bullet go by me. I got nervous because, at the same time, I saw the Men in Black. I took it all wrong. I told my mother on the phone about the different things I had thought, but when I went to look into the hole, they told me different and very interesting things. There was a man on the floor, and there was one with the V above him, and a couple of others, There was another man in front of the one on the floor. His hand was moving up and down so fast, and he said to me, "Look at my friend." The impression I got was that one of our people had done that to him. I think the V aliens heard me on the phone and corrected me. They sent five men dressed in black, and they all turned around. They had on black jackets that had some kind of writing on the back, but I couldn't make it out. It looked like I was going through some tests.

I fell, but then I was sitting down, and I felt a big breeze, as if there was a construction fan in front of me. It blew my hair back, and the upper side of my head went a little numb. Was it from the fall or the blowing of the fan? I fell, and my whole back went out of whack.

Then a while back, I was upset and crying. I didn't know whether I was coming or going. The tissue I was using formed into designs. It was so beautiful; they made a girl with tears coming down her face, as if they were telling me not to cry.

That's the feeling I got at the time. I did not know who was coming after me; I didn't know if it was people. But the minute I got hold of real TV shows, it was like everything started. They warned me to be brave. The V warned me; they told me as clear as someone next to me, "Be brave." And everyone would know but me that a friend had said ugly things about me, or said I was shy and didn't want to talk to anyone. I knew they can follow you and make money off you. Damn, that really got me mad, and someone else was trying to use my name. I wasn't too fond of that. We only have one name, and for someone to say she was me really ticked me off. You'd think people would love to have their own lives instead of trying to be people they're not, I'm not perfect and don't present myself as being perfect, so who in the world would want to portray me? With all the things I went through, I thought I was losing my mind for a minute. I would not want anyone to go through what I went through. I didn't ask for this -to be born like this -but I feel this is my gift and would like to learn more about it. As for seeing the V taking their pictures and the parallel worlds, it feels strange walking outside and not seeing my friends flying around when I don't see them. I say, "Where are you?" And one pops up.

I mentioned my birthmark that I always thought of as a plane, and when I started seeing all this again, I looked on my body for some marks. And this birthmark I had, when I looked at it again, it was perfect rectangles -a perfect shape. The other marks were of three circles on my left leg.

Later on, I looked again in the hole, and they showed me so many things -people by the hill and people lowering people down a hill. It look so real as I watched them, and I saw an older couple with their hands in the air. I didn't know if they were clapping or what, but I thought something didn't look right. People were lowering people down a rope on the side of the hill, and on the other side, it looked like a lot of bodies. What was going on? Well, that couple looked like a senior couple that I'd seen on the side. When I looked the other way, there was an alien wearing the old Roman uniform. It was all black and completely covered his face. He had some kind of space gun on him, and he was standing in front of that couple with a gun on them. Now there were different races. It looked like a war was going on. There were mountains over there. It looked like they had volcanoes at one time. I felt so helpless. I saw everyone in the room -JC and all the kids and family were in a room that was all cluttered. They needed help. There was something wrong with their mountains. They were all so cluttered in a room there, and I could tell they needed help. I wondered, "If their mountains are bad, and they're having trouble with them, and if we are parallel to them, what could happen?" I saw they had fire stations just like ours. They had masks on.

CHAPTER 9

They showed me the month of April 2013, but I didn't know what that meant. My family walked in, and it was a sight. My mother asked if talked to them, and I said, "No, Mom, I'm just looking." One day, though, I was on the phone with her, and I went to the hole. They told me I was rare, and they showed me every step of my life and that JC had been next to me. I like to think of him as my guide and guardian angel, because the Lord knows there have been times when I've gotten into accidents and shouldn't have been here.

At first, it seemed like we were reading each other's minds. I kind of like it that way. I would nod my head if they nodded. That's how we communicated, using a lot of common sense. When they showed me my Native American family, they came out in full regalia, with headdresses and beautiful Native American outfits. My father came out, and my mother was there, When I was attacked by so many groups out here, it got kind of crazy. I felt like everyone was after me, and there was no one to turn to, like everyone went against me. I don't know why -I've never done anything to them. The ones I thought would be next to me weren't there. It was sad; just when I was regaining trust, I got smacked in the face. I guess it was an awakening, showing who my friends are and who is not. From what I saw, they wanted to make a fast buck. I don't know, because for sure, I heard -as clear as day in my ears -"book will be June 1," and it was a lady.

I noticed when I put some video on the Internet that all kinds of UFO groups tried to reach me in their own way. I wouldn't advise anyone to meditate, not unless you know what's coming. When I needed spiritual help, I called my father, mom, and grandma, and they came fast.

In April 2013, they showed seven moons, and in front of them were three more, round like planets. One was small, the middle one was big, and the next was small. They were in a line together in a angle. The next photo was of a girl on the side. She looked like she was in hay and writing or painting. She writes down abbreviations and numbers and letters. Another man, I call Grandpa V, and this one is named JC.

I think his name is JR, but I call him JC. He can hold something in his hands, and aim toward him, and show you exactly what you ask him about. They are so intelligent, advanced on a consciousness level. He can go back in time and to the future. It seems like they watch TV on us, like it's our thoughts in every minute and second in our minds, like it's their TV or something to do with tests. They told me to be brave, but I felt so paranoid or got a really fast feeling that is hard to explain, like my whole life was flying by in front of me on a really fast speed. Just the other day, when I felt that strong breeze in front of me -the one that pushed my head back -it was as if a spirit went through me. It felt like a wave from the beach before it crashed on the shore, when you go up and down as the wave builds up. That's how it feels when a spirit goes through me, or when they cling to me -it's like a feeling of a vibration on me.

I kept feeling the vibration on my side, and I went to the doctor, but he said nothing was wrong with me. Last night, I looked in the hole and saw a boat and poles and people holding them. I figure it's groups trying to communicate, and they're just sending their waves out this way. They think they're reaching them, but it's just reaching me, and I am a chip -a very important chip. They mean I have a chip in me, but I don't really know. I had myself checked out, and I did have a CT scan, and there was no metal in my body, so I don't know what they meant.

They showed me their planet one time -the one I mentioned has an image like a man holding a hammer. It looks like they have two suns, and I have their consolation. A while back, a friend of mine came over and brought a lot of things from around the corner. He said a man lived down the street, but he died, and the police went in there and took some things. This man supposedly worked for NASA. I wish I would have known, so I could have talked to him, but I looked over everything my friend brought over. Some of the things looked like they were meant for me. Two weeks later, I got an e-mail from someone with the same name as the man that had just had passed away. Kind of strange, don't you think? When they told me to be brave, they really meant what they said. They showed me so many things that it's very hard to figure what they mean, but I do know they're V aliens from another world that have different races.

And I've been told they're the oldest race of aliens around. I was told and saw on TV that they're biblical aliens. I don't really like to call them aliens; they're a race, just like us -except, as I've said, for their different skin, which is because of their environment.

When I first started to see them, I thought, *Oh, my gosh. I have just seen what my father and mother have told me*, I was excited and wished my father was here physically, because I know he is here with me. I would have loved to see his face if I showed him the photos of how they take off, but I never would have imagined that we live so close to them, yet so far.

If you have seen my videos, you have seen how they fly right next to us. At first, I was thinking other things, but then I figured it out a little and started to ask them questions. Why next to us? You will see them fly above, next to us, and by our cars and our lights. My theory is that they get energy from our lights. When some people see my videos, they will say, "Oh, they're just lights." But I don't think so. When they fly by themselves and right there in photos, that is not just a light from cars or reflections, but there will always be someone out there to discredit me or people trying to say they are me because they like UFOs.

I know what I take photos of, and computers and cameras don't lie. I stayed quiet for so long, and then when I finally came out, I thought someone would have helped, but no. It was like every time I was on a zoning trip, my sister had to remind me of that. She'd tell me they call it zoning. I'd be looking at my computer, and it would say, "Come to our community group of UFOs."

Anyhow, I really do think they're skin is different from ours because of the environment. Just imagine if we lived on the moon. We would be slinky, with no muscles, and if we lived on Mars, we'd be underground if the planet really is red -or do they just tell us that? I don't know, but I'm sure someone knows. Anyway, when I came out, someone put on the computer that I was not sharing anything of what I know. If my computer wasn't so hacked or played with, I would been letting people know.

As I was saying, they fly right next to us. They just live next to us; we are parallel with them. From what I've seen, we are three feet away from them. They are so intelligent, living on a conscious level, and they are shape-shifters. They shape-shift into anything they want. When they told me how they became who they are, it was so beautiful. They showed me a beautiful bird, a fish, and a dinosaur. They showed me like it was a film of how they became, and they showed me where they live. They live just like us. They have different races, and there is something up with their mountains. They have volcanoes. I saw them trapped in that room, and I was helpless. They're so intelligent -that's the part I see. They're like us in some ways; they still have to figure out their world. But something is going on with their weather, and we're parallel to them. That does tell me about our greenhouse effect. It could mean something's up with that.

CHAPTER 10

When I started to write last year, I was using the dragon, and actually, it works very well, but I always had to stop and reduce it and delete, because when I use the dragon, I'm talking in a mike and dictating everything. Someone was talking through me, telling their own story, and they even put the measurements of their mountains. I kept saying, "Jeez, someone's telling a story." It wouldn't stop, so I stopped. I'll do one soon; I guess you know it's called ghost writing.

So they started showing more of my family dressed in their regalia, and they showed me myself as a little girl, a chubby Native American, sitting in between five ladies. Then they were dancing around me, with their arms moving up and down. Then it switched to where we were sitting. Everyone was there; my grandma was down a ways and singing, and they were playing their drums. They looked like they were having a good time. When they first showed me, they were walking sideways inside the room. Then, the next day, I saw myself in a bath, and some ladies were wiping my arms and cleaning me up. I'd never seen them before, but I imagine they were hybrids. And another time, I was in a classroom with a lot of kids that looked like hybrids -half human. They wrote on the chalkboard in an old European language that I was in an experimental room. The children kind of looked like they were hybrids; they had a cartoonish type of look. The next minute, I was in the air, possibly six feet high, and there was a circle of five boys around me. It seemed like they were meditating as they held me up in the air.

Then when JC came, he was holding a lot of children, and he said they were mine. It was a lot of children; he had a handful of kids. Some days, if I was sad or upset, he would bring the kids to get me in a better mood. And I admit, it did. I would be very excited when he brought the kids over. JC showed me my boy -my son, may he rest in peace, my only boy -with a lot of children. It made me so happy, because he always wanted a lot of kids. When he passed, I said, "Lord, if he lands in V World, let my son meet a nice, kind hybrid and have a lot of children." I think that's exactly what he did. I'm so happy for him. I got to see them the other day. JC showed me that my son had a lot of boys and some girls too.

One thing I do know: when the children from V World are born, they grow fast. It's as if when children in this world are three months old, children in V World are six months old. A one-year-old is like a two-year-old in V World. They grow very fast. They attend school, and they are very intelligent. When I went to see my son at the church, to dress him, as I was on the way there, I saw my son on a cloud, drifting back and forth, with a big heart, saying, "I love you, Mom. Family is here and coming." That day when I saw him, he had that big heart in his arms and looked very happy. That made me feel so good. I usually take photos right away, but I didn't even want to pull out the camera. I wanted to absorb everything, so I just watched that time, looking at my son and not letting go of him. But I do know I'm there with him.

As I've mentioned, they call me VN1, which means special person, and they told me I'm their queen. And when they warned me that day to be brave, they showed me and let me hear the friends of mine that took my information, and they even showed me which ones sold my information. It looked they went to a doctor, and the doctor looked an alien.

I could hear everything. I start singing -I always sang in court tanks and cells and showers. The first time they heard me sing, I heard a person say, "Oh look, our queen sings." And another person said, "Well I'll take her voice." I saw a beautiful woman with blue eyes and all the children. I would always hear that she was with us. She was shy.

I would write to people, and they wouldn't write, I guess they just wanted to steal what I know. I seen a few conferences on people who have been abducted and told their stories. They said they don't talk to UFO TV shows. Now I know why, and I don't blame them. One day, someone told me about throwing ice on my head and that I should drink milk of magnesia because it does a good cleansing. The next day, another person came to my house and told me to do the same thing. So I went shopping. When I got to the store, I parked the car and walked in the store, and lo and behold, there was a pile of ice right by my car and a DVD of songs was in the bushes. As I walked to the store from the parking lot, I grabbed songs from the seventies and Spanish songs. To me, it's no coincidence. At first, the V told me to talk to a lady, but when she got with a friend of mine, they told me no. The V always warn me. My theory is that they show people to talk to me, and I should be careful, because I will be in for a *watusi*. They call it help, but they want to make money off me. Just the other day, someone told me. "I thought maybe you weren't going to push the issue." Funny thing; I called a lawyer, and he sent a detective here to take photos of my house, to see that there is a parallel world connected to me, and that I can see to different areas of the world and they are connected. Luckily, I called and reported it to the news and got a lawyer. They sent it to Orange County. Parallel everything is reported, so there are people out there who claim to be me.

No, you didn't birth me and give me my gift. I call it that, and so do the V. Find the parallel world or however you're putting it to other people, because for sure, if they felt I wasn't going to push it, they should have stopped hacking me or should have talked to me. That doesn't justify what they did to me -they talked to some other person who told them everything I saw or knew, and then said I'm shy. Well. I'm not shy about talking about my V. They should have just talked to me. I put video on the computer of the UFO, along with my e-mail, so anyone could have written to me, instead of saying they are me or that I'm shy.

That's a big lesson for me. I love to wake up and see what that day is going to bring me, and I'm never too old for a new lesson. I'm an easygoing person, down-to-earth, and I get along fast with people. I don't go looking for the unknown; that's not a good idea, unless you know what you're doing.

This is an everyday thing for me. Just two days ago, I was at the store, and the dragon came flying by me. Darn, I had my camera set only on snapshot, and the dragon went flying by me too fast. It was very beautiful. The purple lines in my photos and videos represent the dragon. One time I was driving to pick up my pizza. I was at the stop sign, and flying V saucers were at the stop sign, too, shaped in a perfect V. I grabbed my camera and took the picture. They are red. So I took the photo while I was in the car, and when I looked at it two days later, I was under the dragon's wing. How did that happen?

For me, I know that foil really works on my head to prevent me from hearing any voices or to prevent anyone from hearing me. White hats stop it too and stop the awful headaches when all the groups try to attack me -like UFO groups from our world or different kinds of phenomena groups -when they hear I'm a queen to the V aliens or unidentified flying saucers.

People follow me, or they meditate and try to reach me. I was taking a nap one day, and I heard them chanting my name, trying to get me over there, saying, "Pam -we almost got her." I said a prayer to my Lord, the Lord's Prayer, and afterward, I looked in the hole and saw a bunch of kids from our world, sliding into a pool. Then I saw myself drift above them. I'm not a church person. I was raised to believe I can talk to God wherever I am. One thing my mom always told me was that I had to be cleansed too. I know that. But I've learned through my experience that our God talks to me in any shape or form or however my mentality is at the time. My V know that I'm a child of God, and they accept me how I am. I accept them and embrace the gifts they gave me. I used to be scared to pass away, but now I'm happy to know that when I go from this world, I will enter the other world. I know these parallel worlds and that I'm there already,

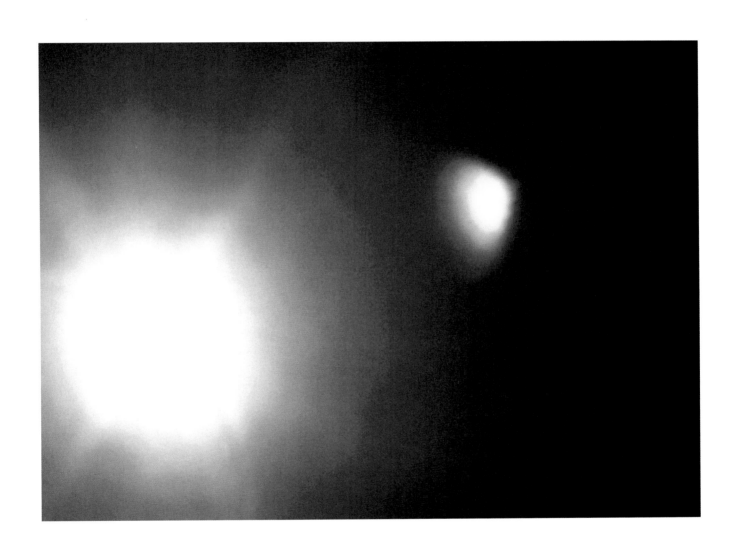

CHAPTER 11

One night JC and I sat together at my dining room table and had a conversation. He talked really fast, like a serpent dragon. His mouth was moving so fast; it was letters moving fast. I had to put it in a slow motion to read the letters. I saw last night that they put PAM = LOVE. I think that was very nice of them. I've seen a mountain carved of me, looking sideways, like I was asleep. I really do believe that they are preserving our human race. The Men in Black mean no harm. They showed me an important person of theirs on the floor. And one of my friend aliens showed me, with his hand moving very fast up and down, "Look at my friend -what they did to him." It seemed to me that this person -a friend of theirs or family of theirs -seemed very important and that someone of our human beings hurt him or something happened. And they were very sad because of that. I've seen the Men in Black, and they've never done anything bad to me. The TV shows do portray how they look -what I have seen, they look like that.

When I asked them about their mountains, they told me of the volcanoes. I'm sure something was wrong with their mountains. They were very excited when I mentioned the Anunnaki. I think they have something to do with the Anunnaki. They speak English very well and understand it very well, and there always are ladies on the phones, like operators. And they keep telling me to sage my house. I have a feeling it's because Gramps V came back, and maybe he didn't like what he saw at other places or didn't like what they were doing to me. I not sure. But I saw when he walked into a house, and now he's back. He's a nice man in his sixties or seventies, and when I take my photos, he's with me most of the time. He will warn me if someone's watching me or going to pass me. He's a nice man.

Last night I saw a few around me. And again the next day, a lot of parallels. I know someone sold some stuff and pictures of mine and some old maps I had, so if anyone sees photos of mine, let me know. They're sentimental to me. There's even my name under search engines -at least they said my name and it was mine -but I haven't received any money for it. It looks like a lot of girls are pretending to be me. and they're *not*. That's why they had to steal my photos and stuff, and they're getting money for the credit of my gift. They call it V TV, and everyone wants to get involved, and they make people pretend they're me, and they receive money for it. I think Grandpa V maybe got angry about that; maybe that's why he left their place, because he always wanted to warn me not to see a certain person. I do know this, and they showed me a jail and prison there.

They have law and order over there, just like our world, so I think if they don't get caught up here, they will be there. The other night I went out to see the asteroid, and when I walked out, they showed me a red ball, like it was on fire, toward the northeast. There are always ladies on the phone, and the strings hanging down. They have the portal. It looks like a willow, with the red lines going around the wheel. That's how their portal looks where people come through, like they're waiting in line. I believe they are saving our race. They are giants or tall, and we are smaller than they are. Those are the V biblical UFO, but then again, there a lot of other races. There are different races than ours. I've seen where their reproduction is. I'm not quite sure. but I've seen a lot of people walking out of a hole into another one, and the process moves like through another person coming out of the mouth of another, down toward their stomach, up toward the left. And they say to hum, I think. I had mention this, but things still go on like last night. Someone said they were going to blow my head off. I don't know if someone sent them after me or if someone just got paranoid around me. I don't know/

I guess that goes with the program of living in parallel worlds. It's kind of scary not knowing when someone is going to pop up in front of you and want to blow your head off because they don't like what you shared with the public or that you're not sharing, so you're kind of screwed either way. One time, they put on the Internet that I wasn't sharing.

Last night, they showed some of the photos of what they'd been showing. They always showed a cross figure, or it could have been a bird figure. The other night, they showed me Jesus on the cross. It was as if I was watching the whole thing over again, from what I've seen on TV, off the Lord being persecuted.

Strange -then it started to show clouds around it, and then the owl came again. Later, they showed some old Hebrew writing. I had to put foil on my head, and it helped for a minute, but I could still hear what was going on. I didn't know if it was our people or theirs. The other day, Danny and I were reading the rules of a book, and I walked up to him at about 11:00 p.m., and before we knew it, it was 3:00 a.m. And later, I looked in the window and saw all the aliens around us, reading my paper. Were Danny and I knocked out and put to sleep? I don't know.

CHAPTER 12

We lost some time. It looked like maybe we could have been abducted. I'm not sure if I want to be hypnotized, because I hear it's better not to do it. Then again, I consider my UFO friends as guardian angels. They do warn me when someone is after me. I would not advise anyone to check out the mysteries of UFOs unless they know what they're doing or study them for a while. Last night, three of us heard what sounded like a freight train going through my living room. It woke us up. At the same time, I was having a dream of trucks, so I don't know if I was half there and we heard them drive by. That's how it is, living in this parallel world.

Another time, I was looking in the window and saw black things aiming at me. I took off, thinking they were going to shoot me, but no -they were taking pictures of me. So I peeked back, and the next thing I knew, I was posing for them, smiling. I guess everyone gets scared when they see them. They don't give them a chance to communicate.

One day, I took a lot of photos of them in the tree, and I saw a cop go by. Well, in my rebel days, we called them "pigs." It slipped out -I said, "Man, look at all the pigs down the street. I wonder what happened." I should have explained what it meant, because JC, my guardian, said, "How dare you call us pigs? I brought them out here to see you."

I felt bad and had to explain to him that that's what I called a cop back in my rebel days; then they understood. So they're very intelligent, but sometimes I have to explain things to them. I explained that some people may lash out at times when they're angry, but they don't mean what they say at the moment. Then I told them there are meanings to words, which I get out of our dictionary. I do I explain a lot simple things, but I love to ask them of our history.

The other night, I asked them about our pyramids in Egypt -how they were made. They showed me a ladder going to the sky and gods, They showed our people making them and tall people helping and shaping the blocks, and it looked like they were raising their hands toward the sky. It looked like a tornado, in a way, shaped the pyramids. It was like water too, as if that part was underwater at some time and easy to put together. Then a ladder went up to the heavens.

A ball came out, and they showed that the ball opened up, and a photo showed what I'd asked. One night, I woke up at two in the morning. My right side could not move -it was paralyzed. Something told me to urinate on my arm, and then, all of a sudden, my arm started to move. I think that was an old ancestry medicine that worked for me.

I see writing everywhere; it's like everything is connected to this world, like everything has its own soul. Writing shows up everywhere. I have a stigmata when my guardian wants to tell me that someone is after me. I'll start itching on my inner arm, and the photo of a person will show up and the person's name. JC has warned me that I was being poisoned. I put the food in my mouth after I read that, but it was for real. The skin on the top of my mouth just came off. Then my arm was itching more, and the photo came out with the person's name. I don't know why I put it in my mouth; I just had to see if it was true, and it was. It was a human instinct, a dumb one. I should have listened. When I get that stigmata, it's like it's bona fide. There are two oracles in the hole that tell me, but it's hard sometimes to make out what they say.

I was getting texts from people after I heard in my head that someone was texting me, telling me everything of what was going on. I'm talking about how you get paranoid. If you're abducted, and you don't know what's coming at you, you start hearing voices. But they warned me and told me that people would be playing games. Sure enough, the names they wrote were my friends. I can thank the one who texted me and told me it was not just me. It could be the government. They want it to look like a conspiracy, so you won't believe what you see.

I think from the beginning, our government should have told us. It's a touchy matter, because some people just can't take things. Now, even in 2014, it seems like we're far but really, we're not. I mentioned how we live together and that we're actually three to five feet away, parallel to them. One day, my guardian was reaching out to me. It's all conscious living. As for talking to each other, they move things with their minds, but maybe it's a little telekinesis.

One day I was going to sage the hole I look into, and I saw tigers and a lot of different animals. I think they were doing their shape-shift. I got a little weary, so I went to get some sage. And they said, "No. Why are you doing that? We live together." They kept saying that I lived with them, and they started to disappear. So I told them I would not sage, and they reappeared. There are some spirits here too. There is one name Ivey. I called her, and she appeared. She is a young girl about ten years old. She holds a little doll and reminds me of those raisins that sing. That's how some of them look -they shape into anything and everything. They do a lot of testing, like how mad we get. Then our government does their thing, and there you go, on a chase. I do know they use my so-called friends and offer them money. I guess the things I went through was too much of a coincidence, but then again, JC, my guardian, told me they would be playing with me. That's when I started to hear people in my head, It was JC telling me and showing me the other people, and he said to be brave. When I started to sing, I heard, "Oh, I'll take her voice." As for the other people that were stealing or pretending to be me, JC told me that they got black-balled, because they had been lying the whole time, either saying they were me or that I was a really bad person.

I think the government or someone goes in your house and puts up cameras or tape recorders. And with all the music I've been singing and making, they make albums, or I could be on a reality show in foreign countries and not even know it. I don't think they should do that; after all, it is my life story of my past life -how I'm rare and have been queen in my past life. It's an invasion of my privacy, without even being invited and making money off me. Things that happen in the city -all the raids and other stuff of the poor -they just change the dates, names, and there you have their script. And people are poor, and they take the other person's side. They just met for money or sex, whichever suits them, not thinking of their friendship or how they might feel about it. They helped them when they needed help, but they tend to forget, and the people with whom they choose to get involved and give money to them only came around for money. The people they gave money to hardly see them, except when money was around. And the rich get richer off us.

There will be people you grew up with that knows the whole thing, because they got a piece of the pie, and it's always someone close to you. Money makes people change. They do crazy things, and they choose to go against you. The ones who get abducted use your friends against you. And the alien TV shows I tried to call -the ones who were making money off me -were hitting every resource, and they knew about me already with their tapes and cameras, and I'm sure they made a lot of money. And I didn't receive a cent. Karma will get them. They will get theirs. Our world turns with every emotion that runs through us. I won't waste my energy on the friends that screwed me and used me. Their time will come, and I don't want to be around them when it does. I feel this is a gift from God to me.

I'm a messenger; I feel that. The unidentified flying objects are the V biblical aliens. And as long as I keep seeing them, I'm going to keep writing of them and taking their photos. The Men in Black are friendly. I have a lot of photos of them. They've been nice to me. I've run up to them many times, and they don't attack me. I think I scared them one time when I first saw them. I ran up to them and told them I was tired of their following me. Then they just looked at me with a nonchalant look on their faces and then disappeared. Later, they told me the whole story. I met a few of them, and they said no one gives them a chance. Everyone runs and screams, "Oh my gosh! Aliens, aliens!" I'm sure a lot of people heard of different things, like VTV -that they watch us for their entertainment. Everyone has a thought, and thoughts are running through everyone's head. Let's say you wake up and go to work, and a car cuts you off. You get mad, so some people say you're an idiot -that's one thought. Number two thought is, *How would you like it if I did that to you?* And number three thought: *I'm going to smash your car.* So what they do is entertain themselves on their VTV by watching our thoughts, Different things that people think are pretty crazy. Our thoughts when we are mad are like a horror movie to them. So when they are at the movies, I see them getting up and getting popcorn and crossing over the people to the snack shop.

I can see them literally get up, as if I'm in the back of the movie show, watching in the background. I see them pass on the streets -the hybrid aliens, different races -as well as sitting down to watch VTV. They don't do that all day, though. They go to work, and their kids go to school. They learn very fast. They drive right next to us in the cities; they live just like us. I think when they first came around us, at that time they should have started living with us,

CHAPTER 13

The other day, I was going to sage my house with sage grass. It's a grass a Native American uses to cleanse houses for prayer. You might remember that they told me not to do it -some like it, but some don't, so I told them the sage would not hurt them. It was a good thing and wouldn't cause negative things or do bad things.

A little girl hybrid disappeared first, I watched her fade away when I saged, and then she came back. Now I tell them when I'm going to sage. In the middle of my living room, there was a set of TV equipment that worked like a studio, and they were filming me. They filmed me cooking, and I explained to them what I was cooking and the ingredient and how it was healthy. And I have all the V kids here in my living room. Most of them are like my children.

The other day I was looking at my sand, and a set of eyes poked up, and a little man came out with his hands wide open. I asked him if he wanted his picture taken. Maybe I should have taken it, but I didn't. I told him that the next time I saw them with their wheelbarrows and shovels, I'd take their pictures.

I was watching our astronauts on the History Channel, and they said when they have seen saucers in space, they had a dome on them. And the V UFOs that I saw had domes on top of their saucers.

I am dealing with different paranormal groups attacking me. And it's nothing nice. Some people drop off mail, asking if I'm okay, but they must drive by and drop it in my mailbox, because it's not in a envelope; it's just a note. If they really cared, they would talk to me in person, or maybe they just don't want to get involved. Maybe it's the government just trying to make me think it's some kind of conspiracy and not UFOs.

When you get abducted, you do hear some voices, but you wonder if it's your people from earth, plotting. Are they being paid to mess with you? Or is it from the other planet? I come in and say some prayers to send them away. I don't know why, but they go around your people, and they take some money to do whatever against you. I've seen myself on the floor, and they were marking me with X's on my arms and legs. I think they were marking to see where there were chips. I guess it would be metal parts to UFOs. I've gotten MRIs and CT scans and nothing shows up.

And there is a portal to someone else's house. It looks like it, but it's really the reflection of my house. The other paranormal groups attack me, or they will meditate and try to come in my house. They called it VTV, and then they sold it to make money, and it was only a reflection of my house. I saw them in a hole, the V UFO, and they wrote and talked to me. It's like a TV; that's how it looks when I'm looking at it' And groups just keep trying to come in, and I say some prayers so they go away.

The other day, I went to the backyard. Someone put a lot of slugs under a pot. It did not look normal, so I know someone had been messing with me. I found some burned orange peelings, or someone burned something on my barbecue. And I don't know why, but they started to show some photos the other day. It's a man; it looks like maybe a high school photo.

A group started to follow me around, and the V showed me some owls and mathematical equations. I think a lot of it has to do with numbers. I was told to pay attention to numbers when someone get abducted. My husband and I got abducted. We were on the couch, and they were looking over a lot of paperwork. They did nothing wrong to us. I do know they're so advanced that they could just unzip a body like a sweater. They showed me that before. I don't know if it was one of them in a suit or if it was one of us, but it kind of looked like it was one of us.

Later, I saw myself grabbing my husband out of a volcano hole in our living room, so these earthquakes kind of make me wonder. Maybe we have a volcano in our house in the bottom. Maybe the aliens showed me that to tell me there was a earthquake coming. They told me the other day that my son was crossing over, and I just kept telling him, "I'm with you, *mijo*. Everything is okay. Follow the light," I was so happy to see him. It looked like he was walking up a pyramid to the heavens, and a lot of people were behind him, and a light was in a distance. I'm glad we were together. I know he felt me.

I feel I'm a messenger for them, but the only thing is, I get really bad headaches. My ears ring, and when other people found out about me, I don't know who was kicking me to the side -my people or the Aliens. They like pizza and hamburgers and popcorn and cheese And they love music. They talk with colors, and they spell the letters in their mouths. When I look at them, and they're talking to me, a letter will appear in between their lips,

And their lips move fast. On one of the photos, I have a scene were they have their chariots. If you look on YouTube where I put my video, this is the one that says "sign moves well in the tree." There is a picture of their chariots -flying saucer. Didn't the Bible say there were flying chariots? They have photos of it in a museum, and in every film they put a V in it, but in this world, they also have a lot of rats in different sections, and the speed is fast.

I was filming a horse at the corner one day, and it was running in place and fast. Then all of a sudden, they showed a huge ball rolling down the sidewalk, and all of a sudden, little ones came out of it. Then they switched to flying in the middle of the street, and a big saucer came. This time there were not big balls; the saucers came and went in the middle of the street. And then, just like the big ball, a bunch of little ones came out of it and flew fast.

If I saw my son crossing the other day, does that mean it takes eight months for people to cross? It's strange, though. I told them I was almost done with the book and asked if there was anything they wanted me to say. That's when they said my son was crossing. They gave me a feeling as though if I did something good for them, I got something in return. One thing I did wrong -and I asked for forgiveness for interrupting, his journey -was that I asked my son a question, and he flew down the stairs. I felt bad and told him to stop. I said that I was okay and that he should keep going to the light. I kept praying for him and telling him to follow the light. I've been telling him that since he was a little boy -that when he goes, he and everyone will follow the light. I showed him how to cleanse his aura all the time, and he saw the aliens, but he would say, "If they have a social security number, then tell me, Mom." And he would laugh.

When he saw the ones I put on the website, he wondered a lot, and I always told JC to go slow with him. I think he had to fight, for some reason, when he left, and landed in V World. I know he was there. I heard someone telling him the night he passed. I actually heard someone's voice telling my son the directions to that planet. I heard them say to go around Orion's Belt. And when I saw him fighting, that got me upset. And I told my aliens that he was my son, of my blood. I said, "You treat him with respect, because if I know my boy, he would do the same to you." He was the type to give his last jacket to someone. So I asked JC to take care of him and show him around, and he did.

He was fighting other races there. There are some so jealous of me, because the V treat me very nicely. There is a war going on over there right now with the Kemens race and the Yemens. There is another one too. Maybe that's what he was fighting about, but he's fine now. He is on his way to heaven now. The aliens are saving our race; that's how I see it, by the way they show me things. They're like a reproduction section. They save some people, and I don't know how they pick, but what I've seen is that they pick all our races. And like being reborn. You come back again and again -something my dad told me. Everyone comes back to redo life over and over again, to reach their peak of awareness. That's what they have been showing me in the holes and my past lives and future. It's interesting, because they'll show every thought of mine for their VTV. They threw a party for me one time, and another time they showed this huge film. It looked like the drive-in theater. A man was giving a speech.

I saw a woman giving a speeches all the time, but her back always faced me, and she looked like me from the back. Tonight some other paranormal group tried to cover the VTV. It only lasted for a while, but that's just one window that opened up. There's a lot of them. I have to cover them up. Last night a UFO flew in front of my house; it was huge and red.

A couple of years ago, the different races had meetings and everything seemed okay, but someone bombed their reproduction portal on their planet. They had fire engines there. People were hurt, and that was the portal that people came through for being reborn.

It's really hard to understand that your people and friends that actually burned you and had other people pretend they're you. It's the aliens producing three or seven of you, and they're showing a film on you in their world. Actually, I think that is what makes a lot people, something like cloning -they produce bodies when someone passes on, and then they'll send the person crossing over to the next level.

The other day my foot was hurting, and I got a rash. JC wrote on the floor and told me what was wrong with me, so I got sage and put it under my feet. And what a difference. It felt so much better. The swelling went down, and the pain went away.

CHAPTER 14

It seemed like JC was warning me about what was happening to me, and it looked like I was getting attacked by another race. The way everything came down, it was as if he was warning me of another race. When I bring the priest in, and he sprinkles holy water all over my house -the backyard, the shack, each room, me, and my animals -the big heads leave, which are the Gray Aliens. I saged really good the other day, and there was a cheetah here. But then again, in my dome, when I take photos, there is always a cheetah or lion. Don't forget, they are shape-shifters. Some have a possum face and a turkey tail; the others look like gulls, and others look old, with no expression, and some cackle loudly. They were very stubborn the other day when I saged, but some of them finally left. I told them if they were not here for good, "then leave -you're not wanted," and all the little children hybrids stayed here.

I don't want them to scare the children away. When I saged, I caught a wolf over an alien. It's the second time I caught that on tape. I think the wolves are protecting me, because in one photo, there is a wolf on my shoulder. And oil keeps dripping; first some oil would come out of me, and now it's dripping down my blinds. I had them cleaned, or it could be I'm sweating it out.

As for the races not getting along, I've seen treaties from before, and now, they write others, and a lot goes into their words. I think their words mean a lot. They have mathematical meanings, and physics has a lot to do with it. The whole world turns together with one breath; everything is connected. It all comes down to the point that someone made us, our God, which is everyone's God.

The other day I watch the eclipse, and I got a photo of the UFO and the eclipse together when I did the moving camera on it. The eclipse energy was so strong that it pushed the UFO aside. As I was looking at the eclipse, it turned into colors flashing on the moon. The whole moon was flashing different colors. And sometimes the aliens talk with colors, and colors mean numbers, so there might be something there.

I came inside and asked JC if the planets would talk with colors. He said yes, and what was so strange was that the eclipse was red, the moon was red, and the other planet Mars was facing it. And at the same time, there was a light around Mars, and it kept flashing toward the moon, the eclipse.

The light was wrapped around the Mars and open from the side and aimed at the moon. I know there are four planets -I was looking for them.

I'll be writing more on the paranormal activities in my life, my guardians, and the little people. There also are fairies, dragons, and unicorns. They shape-shift. They are the biblical aliens. The first word they told me was "Ezekiel," the word out of the Bible. I don't like to call them aliens. When I say the word "alien," it reminds me of someone being outcast. I feel they are us, and we are of the same.

We all have the gift of the third eye. We just have to learn how to use it. I think God would not have given it to us if we were not supposed to use it. They manifest things so they can live, like items they need. We go to the store for certain items, but they manifest theirs.

They like hamburgers and pizza, and when I came home, they ate it too and liked it. They made it grow in their world -that's how they go shopping. The item has to be new and unused, and they grow another one and use it.

The other day I saw a program on aliens that said people hear voices after they get abducted. That's true, but is it our government or our people? Or the UFOs, just plain old VTV? I kept feeling a vibration on my back. I went to get X-rays, and they did not find anything. A paranormal man mentioned to me that the vibration I was getting on my back was a spirit clinging to me or the UFO. I'm beginning to think that it was the V the whole time -including when I was young and saw the angels on the side of my house -because they are huge and tall.

Some people have had bad experiences, and I do feel for them. Mine has not been a pretty ride the whole time. I've had my good times too. I consider myself lucky to see two worlds, but it's not always a nice walk in the park. Still, I consider myself a messenger.

Say a prayer -that helps the best. They do test after test, and I feel this is my gift. I embrace them. They were given to me from the Ancient Ones, V, and God at the retreat -a Christian prophecy. A lot more religions were there -Jewish, Catholic, and a lot more. It was amazing. I loved what I saw when I opened the Bible that night. They said to me that I have seen what most prophets would love to see in a lifetime.

I love waking up every day, seeing where my journey will take me. I have a spiritual guide who is wonderful and special to me. I pray a lot to our God, and I told them that I'm a child of God, and they understand. They told me I'm their VN1, special person around the world, sweet queen, CYO. Now they call me the Virgin Rose. I think they call me that because my middle name is Rose.

Printed in the United States
By Bookmasters